The PRESSED FLOWER Companion

A Journey from Hobbyist to Artist

SARAH BEXLEY

TABLE OF CONTENTS

Introduction. 5

Meet The Author 9

1. The History of Flower Pressing 13

2. The Science Behind Flower Pressing 17

3. Flower Language and Symbolism;
    The Unspoken Messages of Blooms 21

4. The Surprising Benefits of Flower Pressing 27

5. Beginners: The Easiest Flowers to Press Using a
    Wooden Flower Press. 33

6. Beginners: How to Press Flowers
    for Preservation 43

7. The Best Paper to Help You Press Flowers 49

8. How Long Does It take to Press Flowers?. 57

9. Pressing Flowers in a Book 63

10. Pressing a Rose Petal by Petal 69

11. Wooden vs. Microwavable Flower Presses 75

12. Achieving a Bug-Free Pressed
    Flower Masterpiece 79

13. How To Preserve Pressed Flowers 83

14. Sealing Pressed Flowers to Protect Them. 91

15. Pressed Flowers and Artificial
    Color Enhancement. 97

16. How to Make Dried Flower Confetti At Home. 105

17. Craft Ideas for Pressed Flower Projects 117

18. Top Five Crafty Gift Ideas for
    Pressed Flower Lovers .125

19. Common Challenges in Flower Pressing 131

20. FAQ – Quick Reference Guide to Flower Pressing. . . 137

Conclusion: The Journey Continues 141

INTRODUCTION

*H*ello, fellow flower enthusiast!

If you're reading this, it's likely we share a common love for the delicate beauty of flowers and the joy of transforming them into lasting art. If that's the case, you've found the right book. If you're new to this world, welcome - I'm thrilled to introduce you to the art of flower pressing.

My name is Sarah, and I've been in your shoes. I remember holding my first flower press, feeling both excited and overwhelmed. So many questions buzzed in my mind, like "Which flowers should I press? How long does it take? How can I preserve their stunning colors?" Over time, I've found the answers to all these queries and more, learned from my mistakes, and discovered a passion I never expected to have.

This book, *The Pressed Flower Companion*, is a compilation of all the knowledge I've gained throughout my journey. It's the book I wish I'd had when I started; a comprehensive guide, yet friendly and easy to digest. I will guide you from the absolute beginnings of flower pressing to more advanced techniques and crafty projects.

We'll explore the history of flower pressing, dive into debates about the best pressing methods, and tackle the art of preserving not only flowers but also their vibrant colors. You'll discover the easiest flowers for beginners to press and how to navigate toward a bug-free, pressed flower masterpiece. We'll even delve into creative ideas for your pressed flowers, from home décor to delightful gifts.

This journey is all about patience, creativity, and the joy that comes from producing something beautiful from nature. Whether you're a seasoned flower presser or a blossoming novice, there's something for everyone in these pages.

So, grab your favorite flowers, open your press, and let's embark on this beautiful journey together. Welcome to the enchanting world of flower pressing!

Enjoy,

Sarah xxx

MEET THE
AUTHOR

*H*ello, I'm Sarah!

Like many of you, I find joy and serenity in the simplest things in life - a well-brewed cup of tea, a walk in the park, a cozy reading nook, and, of course, the beauty of nature that unfolds in our gardens and wild spaces.

I'm a proud mom of two beautiful children and a fervent lover of all things creative. I hold a college degree, but my education didn't stop there. My curiosity and love for learning propelled me to explore everything from arts and crafts to gardening and interior design.

I've always had a knack for seeing the extraordinary in the ordinary. Perhaps that's what drew me to flower pressing. The concept of preserving the fleeting beauty of nature fascinated me, and the wooden flower press became my cherished tool.

Over the years, my weekends became filled with garden explorations, art galleries, museums, and, yes, flower pressing. My home now boasts a range of art pieces, each reflecting a moment of nature captured in time. And I've found great joy in gifting these pieces to friends and family and sharing a slice of nature's magic with them.

I believe in authenticity, quality, and patience, virtues I've found indispensable in the world of flower pressing. And now, I aim to share all I've learned with you through *The Pressed Flower Companion: A Journey from Hobbyist to Artist*. This book is more than a guide; it's a piece of my heart, a glimpse into my journey, and, hopefully, a spark to ignite your love for preserving the timeless beauty of flowers.

Let's create, learn, and preserve together!
Happy pressing,

Sarah

THE HISTORY OF FLOWER PRESSING

"The flower that blooms in adversity is the most rare and beautiful of all." —Walt Disney

*F*lower pressing has been an enjoyable craft for hundreds of years. Its simplicity and affordability have made the activity available to all people, no matter their wealth.

The results of flower pressing are exquisite. Many species of flower can be preserved and displayed in a variety of ways and for many different reasons.

Flowers have long been exchanged by lovers as a sign of affection, and the art of flower pressing means these gifts of love can be kept long after the initial flowers would have perished.

But where did flower pressing originate from, and how has it changed over time?

Flower pressing, an art as delicate as it is enduring, is deeply rooted in our history. It's a practice that holds memories, tells stories, and celebrates the beauty of nature. Today, let's travel back in time to explore the origins of this captivating craft.

ANCIENT BEGINNINGS

The earliest record of plant preservation, which is the foundation of flower pressing, goes back to ancient Egyptian times. Egyptians were known for their reverence for plants and flowers in particular. These were not just aesthetically pleasing elements to them; they symbolized life and resurrection. They used to bury their deceased with floral wreaths, as seen in some of their surviving artifacts and tomb paintings dating back to 4000 BC.

THE HERBARIUM TRADITION

Fast-forward to the Middle Ages, when the concept of preserving plants took on a more scientific angle in the form of 'herbaria.' These were collections of plants that were dried, pressed, and then affixed to sheets of paper with notations of their classifications and uses. The practice was primarily used by herbalists, botanists, and physicians for medicinal and scientific purposes. One of the oldest herbaria, dating back to 1532, is housed in the Natural History Museum, London.

THE VICTORIAN ERA: A TIME OF FLOWER FERVOR

The Victorian era from 1837-1901 witnessed a surge in the popularity of flower pressing in Europe, especially among women. This period was characterized by a societal fascination with nature. This, combined with the wealth of exotic plant species brought back by explorers from their voyages, fueled the practice of flower pressing as a pastime. It was during this time that 'Flower Language' or 'Floriography' emerged, where different flowers and arrangements were used to convey secret messages.

Victorian women spent hours collecting, pressing, and arranging flowers into 'Flower Albums.' These albums, as well as being decorative artifacts, acted as a testament to a woman's skill, patience, and appreciation for beauty. Queen Victoria herself was known to have a fondness for flower pressing.

THE ART FORM TODAY

In the modern age, flower pressing has evolved and transcended cultural and geographic boundaries. It continues to be a way for us to connect with nature, preserve a moment in time, and create. It has found its way into various creative outlets, from arts and crafts and DIY projects to high fashion. Alexander McQueen's Spring 2007 collection, aptly named 'Sarabande,' showcased beautiful dresses adorned with pressed flowers.

However, the essence of flower pressing remains unchanged: the joy of capturing the ephemeral beauty of a bloom, the patience and anticipation in the pressing process, and the delight in revealing the pressed treasure.

Today, with the rise of sustainable living and the DIY movement, flower pressing is experiencing a resurgence. Pressed flowers are used in home décor, handmade gifts, and even in mental wellness practices as a form of therapeutic art.

IN CONCLUSION

The history of flower pressing is a fascinating journey, a testament to our enduring fascination with the natural world's beauty. From ancient Egypt's tombs to Victorian England's parlors to our modern-day living rooms and design studios, flower pressing has traveled through time, adapting, and evolving. It has left an indelible mark on our history, art, and culture. And as we continue to press flowers, we also continue to write this history, one bloom at a time.

THE SCIENCE BEHIND FLOWER PRESSING

"Flowers are restful to look at. They have neither emotions nor conflicts." —Sigmund Freud

$\mathcal{F}$lower pressing may seem like a simple hobby involving just a few materials and steps, but a fascinating scientific process is at play underneath its creative exterior. As we delve into this chapter, let's uncover the science behind flower pressing that allows us to preserve the beauty of blooms in a new, timeless form.

THE PROCESS OF DESICCATION

At the heart of flower pressing lies a scientific process known as desiccation, which essentially means removing water. Fresh flowers contain a high percentage of water in their cells, which gives them their characteristic freshness and vitality. However, this moisture is also why they wilt and decompose when detached from the plant.

When we press flowers, we aim to extract this moisture as quickly as possible while maintaining the flower's shape and color. The pressing materials, such as Berstuk blotting paper and weights, help facilitate this. These tools apply pressure to the flowers, squeezing out water and providing a surface for the water to be absorbed into.

The faster this moisture removal occurs, the better the preservation of the flower's form and color. If it's too slow, decomposition processes like mold growth and enzymatic browning may occur. Thus, the art of flower pressing is essentially a race against time.

COLOR PRESERVATION

Color preservation in flower pressing is another fascinating aspect where science takes center stage. The vibrant colors in flowers come from various pigments present in their cells, such as chlorophyll (green), carotenoids (yellow and orange), and anthocyanins (reds and purples).

These pigments are sensitive to factors like light, pH, and temperature. For instance, exposure to sunlight can fade colors due to UV radiation, while high temperatures can break down the pigments. Therefore, fresh flowers tend to fade or change color during pressing, especially if not handled properly.

To mitigate this, it's advisable to press flowers quickly after picking them and store them in a cool, dark place. Some enthusiasts also experiment with techniques like color enhancement using artificial colors or botanical dyes.

THE ROLE OF PLANT ANATOMY

The structure of the flower itself also plays a role in how well it can be pressed. Some flowers are naturally flat or have petals that easily separate and lay flat during pressing, such as pansies or violets. On the other hand, thicker, more succulent flowers like roses may present more of a challenge due to their 3D structure and high moisture content.

Additionally, flowers with naturally darker or more vivid colors, like marigolds or sunflowers, may retain their color better after pressing than more delicate pastel blooms. Thus, understanding plant anatomy and its effects on the pressing process can aid in selecting suitable flowers for pressing and anticipating the results.

THE IMPACT OF EXTERNAL CONDITIONS

Finally, it's important to note the role of external conditions. The environmental circumstances when the flower is picked, such as the time of day and weather, can influence the flower's condition and, thus, the pressing results. For instance, flowers picked on a dry, sunny day will generally have less moisture than those picked after rain or in the early morning, which can make the pressing process quicker and easier.

To sum it up, flower pressing is not just a creative pastime but also a scientific endeavor. Understanding the processes at play can help you become more adept at this craft, anticipate possible challenges, and come up with solutions or adaptations. So, the next time you press a flower, remember you're not just creating art but also engaging in an age-old science experiment! And that's the true beauty of this craft: it's a seamless blend of art and science, of creativity and empirical processes, giving us a unique way to appreciate and preserve the beauty of nature.

FLOWER LANGUAGE AND SYMBOLISM; THE UNSPOKEN MESSAGES OF BLOOMS

"To be overcome by the fragrance of flowers is a delectable form of defeat." —Beverly Nichols

The silent dialogue of flowers has been an important part of human culture for centuries. From conveying clandestine messages of love in Victorian times to representing national symbols today, flowers carry profound symbolism and meanings within their delicate blossoms. In this chapter, we delve deeper into the captivating world of flower language and symbolism, adding an extra dimension to your pressed flower projects.

THE UNSPOKEN LANGUAGE OF FLOWERS: A HISTORICAL PERSPECTIVE

In the romantic Victorian era, the language of flowers, known as 'floriography,' reached its zenith. It was a covert means of communication, allowing individuals to express feelings deemed too passionate, intimate, or controversial for spoken words. Flowers were carefully chosen, their colors meticulously selected, and even the arrangement held significance in the message being conveyed. This coded language added intrigue and depth to courtship and social interaction.

BLOSSOMS AND THEIR MESSAGES: AN EXPANDED EXPLORATION

Let's journey through the enchanting world of diverse flowers and their associated meanings:

▶ **Roses:** The ultimate symbol of love, each rose color has its unique meaning. Red roses are synonymous with romantic love, pink ones denote admiration and sweetness, white roses signify purity and innocence, and yellow roses stand for friendship and joy.

▸ **Tulips**: Representing perfect love, each color conveys a different sentiment. Red tulips embody true love, yellow ones express cheerful thoughts and sunshine, and purple tulips symbolize royalty.

▸ **Daisies**: Symbolizing innocence, purity, and new beginnings, daisies have a joyful energy. In Norse mythology, daisies were Freya's sacred flower, the goddess of love, beauty, and fertility; thus, they are often associated with motherhood and childbirth.

▸ **Sunflowers**: Characterized by their radiant charm and tall stance, sunflowers represent loyalty, admiration, and longevity. Their unmistakable likeness to the sun symbolizes warmth and happiness.

▸ **Lilies**: Depicting purity and refined beauty, different lily types and colors carry varying meanings. White lilies denote purity and virtue, orange ones imply passion, and stargazer lilies represent ambition and encouragement to fulfill dreams.

▸ **Orchids**: These exotic beauties symbolize love, beauty, strength, and luxury. In Victorian England, if a gentleman presented a rare orchid to a lady, it was a declaration of his deep and passionate love for her.

▸ **Carnations**: Generally representing love, fascination, and distinction, each color has specific meanings. For example, red carnations indicate love and admiration, white ones symbolize innocence and purity, and striped ones signify regret or refusal.

▸ **Lavender**: Known for its alluring scent, lavender symbolizes purity, silence, devotion, and caution. In the language of flowers, giving someone lavender means offering them your solemn vow.

- ▶ **Violets**: These lovely flowers are symbols of modesty, spiritual wisdom, faithfulness, and humility. They also carry a message of everlasting love.
- ▶ **Hydrangeas**: These blooms represent heartfelt and sincere emotions, gratitude, understanding, and abundance.

FLOWER SYMBOLISM ACROSS CULTURES - A GLOBAL LANGUAGE

The language of flowers transcends borders, featuring prominently in cultures around the world:

- ▶ In Japan's 'Hanakotoba,' or the language of flowers, blooms like sakura (cherry blossom) signify the ephemeral nature of life, symbolizing a brief period of extreme beauty followed by an equally swift end.
- ▶ In Chinese culture, peonies represent wealth and honor, chrysanthemums stand for long life and rejuvenation, while the lotus, blooming beautifully despite growing in mud, symbolizes spiritual enlightenment in Buddhism.
- ▶ Middle Eastern and Islamic cultures also hold flowers in high regard. Roses, or 'ward' in Arabic, often symbolize love, beauty, and paradise, featuring prominently in Islamic art, poetry, and spirituality.

Knowing the symbolism of flowers allows you to create pressed flower projects that are visually stunning and deeply meaningful. Whether you're creating a personal keepsake, a heartfelt gift, or a commemorative piece, each bloom chosen narrates a story, making your art rich in sentiment and connection. As you collect and press each flower, remember you're preserving more than its outward beauty; you're also capturing its hidden messages and meanings and the essence of its existence.

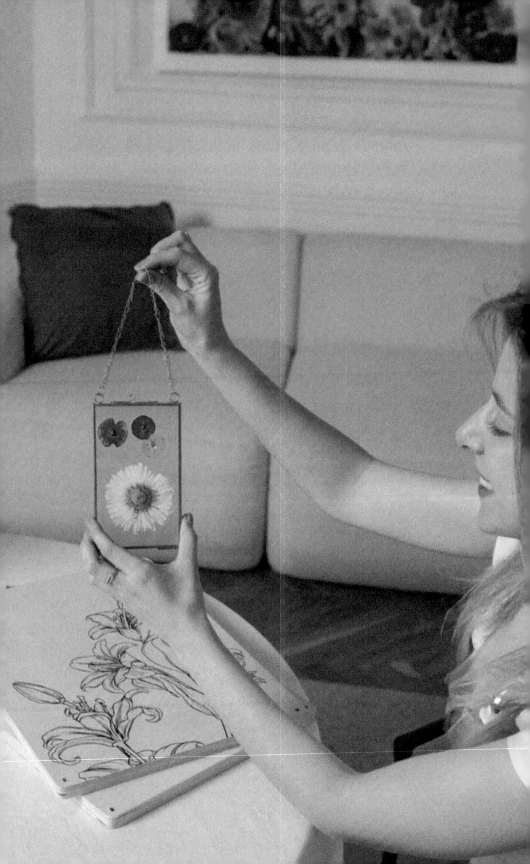

THE SURPRISING BENEFITS OF FLOWER PRESSING

"Flowers don't worry about how they're going to bloom. They just open up and turn toward the light and that makes them beautiful." —Jim Carrey

This simple yet captivating hobby offers a plethora of benefits that will leave you wondering why you haven't picked it up sooner. From preserving the beauty of nature to creating unique works of art and reducing stress, flower pressing has something for everyone. And the best part? It's easy to get started, requires minimal equipment and spending, and can be done from the comfort of your home.

Whether you're a seasoned gardener or someone who simply appreciates the beauty of flowers, here are ten reasons why you should start pressing flowers today.

PRESERVING NATURE'S BEAUTY

One of the most obvious benefits of flower pressing is that it allows you to preserve the beauty of nature in a way that is both simple and long-lasting. Unlike fresh flowers, which inevitably wilt and die, pressed flowers can last for years, providing you with a constant reminder of the natural world.

CREATING ART

Pressed flowers can be used in a wide variety of ways to create beautiful works of art. From simple framed pressed flower arrangements to more complex pressed flower collages and cards, the possibilities are endless. It's a great way to let your creative side shine, whether you're looking to make a unique gift for a loved one or simply looking for a way to decorate your home.

RELIEVING STRESS

Picking flowers, arranging them in a press, and watching them dry over time can provide a meditative and soothing experience. The process is simple, calming, and can be done almost anywhere. It is an easy way to relax and unwind after a long day.

EDUCATING

Pressing flowers is also a great way to learn more about different flowers and their significance in the natural world. As you press different types of flowers, you'll learn about the various shapes, colors, and patterns that are unique to each species, and you'll also learn about the different habitats where they thrive.

LOW-COST HOBBY

Another great thing about flower pressing is that it's a relatively low-cost hobby. You don't need a lot of expensive equipment to get started—all you need is a <u>flower press</u>, which can be purchased inexpensively or even made at home. Once you have your press, you can go out into your backyard or a local park and collect all the flowers you need for free.

MEMORY KEEPING

Flowers represent memories and moments in life. They could be from a special occasion like a wedding or birthday or simply a bouquet from a loved one. Pressing flowers from these special moments can help you keep the memories alive and close to you for a long time. It's a great way to relive the moment every time you look at your pressed flowers collection.

HOME DECORATING

Pressed flowers can be used in a variety of ways to decorate your home. They can be used to create wreaths, garlands, and other decorative items or framed and hung on the wall as art. The natural beauty of pressed flowers can add a unique touch to any room in your home, and they're a great way to incorporate nature into your decor.

PERSONAL DEVELOPMENT

Picking flowers, arranging them, and watching them dry over time can provide a sense of accomplishment. Also, taking the time to create something beautiful can improve your focus, attention to detail, and patience.

ENVIRONMENTAL IMPACT

Picking flowers in the wild can have a negative impact on the environment, but pressing flowers is a great way to appreciate nature without disturbing it. By using flowers that are already dead (cut) or have been grown in a garden, you're not only preserving the beauty of nature but also being mindful of the environment.

GIFT GIVING

Pressed flowers can make great gifts, particularly when they're incorporated into homemade items like cards, bookmarks, or framed art. It's a unique and personal way to show someone you care, and it's also a thoughtful and low-cost gift option.

Flower pressing is a versatile and enjoyable hobby that offers something for everyone. Whether you're looking for a way to preserve the beauty of nature, create art, or simply relax, flower pressing is a great choice. It's easy to get started, and the materials required are inexpensive.

This hobby is a great way to bring a little bit of the outdoors into your home, to learn about the natural world, and to create something beautiful. Plus, it can be a fun activity to do with friends and family, creating a special bonding moment. So, next time you're out for a walk, keep an eye out for beautiful flowers, and give flower pressing a try!

BEGINNERS: THE EASIEST FLOWERS TO PRESS USING A WOODEN FLOWER PRESS

"Just living is not enough... one must have sunshine, freedom, and a little flower." —Hans Christian Andersen

*I*sn't flower pressing the most creative form of art? Pressed flowers make up spectacular frames. They adorn cards and presents with a whiff of elegance. Not to forget the amazing touch of color and beauty added to your aromatic candles, bookmarks, or even paperweights!

However, not all flowers are equally suitable for pressing and preserving. Some flowers are more difficult to press and preserve, while others are much easier to work with. Let's find out which flowers are the best and easiest to press and preserve.

If you are just starting out, begin with the easiest flowers to get your flower pressing game into action!

Here are some insights on the easiest flowers to press using a wooden flower press.

EASIEST FLOWERS TO PRESS

All flowers can be pressed to form the most mesmerizing pieces of art. But there are a few that can promise the best-pressed results!

▶ Flowers with a natural flat bloom
▶ Flowers with a single layer of petals

Here is a list of flowers that can hold their shape and color, making the flower pressing activity super easy:

Pansies

Pansies are one of the easiest flowers to press and preserve for beginners due to their small size and flat petals, which make them easy to work with. They are also relatively sturdy, meaning they are less prone to damage during the pressing process compared to more delicate flowers. In addition to their ease of use, pansies are a great choice for pressing and preserving due to their wide range of colors.

DAISIES

Daisies are another great choice for pressing and preserving. They are relatively flat and have a small number of petals, making them easy to press and preserve. Choose daisies that are not fully bloomed and have a good amount of petals. What could be better than a super flat, pressed-out daisy adorning your bedside table frame?

PS. Many artists will agree that daisies can sometimes be quite challenging because they have very thin petals but thicker centers, which means they will dry at different times. <u>A perfect hack for you is to try and press daisies in between make-up cotton pads. Trust me and just try it :-)</u>

LOVE-IN-THE-MIST

Love-in-the-mist is a great choice for pressing and preserving due to its small size and delicate nature. The flowers are flat and have a small number of petals, making them easy to work with. They are also known for their beautiful blue, purple, or white colors, which add a touch of whimsy to any display or gift. Love-in-the-mist flowers also retain their color and shape well after being pressed.

WILD ROSES (A LITTLE BIT MORE ADVENTUROUS)

Roses are a classic choice for pressing and preserving, and they produce beautiful and delicate results. Choose roses that are not fully bloomed and have a good amount of petals. Avoid using roses that are starting to wilt or have brown edges on the petals.

HYDRANGEAS

Hydrangeas are a stunning and easy choice for pressing and preserving. They retain their vibrant color and delicate appearance well after being pressed. With a range of colors, including blue, pink, purple, and white, hydrangeas add a pop of color to any display or gift. Don't miss out on the opportunity to enjoy the beauty of these flowers for longer by adding them to your pressing and preserving repertoire.

FERNS

Ferns are a unique and beautiful choice for pressing and preserving. They have delicate, feathery fronds that are well-suited for pressing and preserving. Choose ferns that are not fully grown and have a good amount of fronds. Avoid using ferns that are starting to wilt or have brown edges on the fronds.

PRESSED FLOWERS LAST A WHILE

In conclusion, many flowers are suitable for pressing and preserving, including roses, daisies, sunflowers, violets, and ferns. While some flowers, such as orchids and lilies, can be more challenging to press and preserve due to their delicate nature, many other flowers are easy to work with and produce beautiful results. By following a few simple tips and using the right materials, you can successfully press and preserve a wide variety of flowers for display or gift-giving.

These scented lovelies may take weeks to prepare, but they will last for many years! When preserved with care, you can enjoy your masterpieces for many years to come! Though it's always fun to enjoy a fresh batch!

Get started with the easiest ones; you will love the results.

BEGINNERS: HOW TO PRESS FLOWERS FOR PRESERVATION

"The fairest thing in nature, a flower, still has its roots in earth and manure." - D.H. Lawrence

*F*lower pressing is an age-old technique that allows you to preserve the beauty of flowers for a long time. By pressing flowers, you can keep them as a beautiful memory or use them in art and craft projects. In this chapter, we will go over the steps on how to press flowers for preservation.

STEP 1 - PICKING TIME

The first step in pressing flowers is to gather the flowers you want to press. It's best to use flowers that are freshly picked and still in good condition. Avoid using flowers that are wilted or have brown edges, as they will not press well. Some popular flowers to press include roses, daisies, violets, and pansies.

STEP 2 PREP TIME

Once you have your flowers, you will need to prepare them for pressing. Start by removing any leaves, stems, or other debris from the flowers. Then, gently lay them out on a piece of paper, such as <u>blotting paper</u> (my favorite) or printing paper. Make sure to spread the flowers out so that they do not overlap, and gently flatten them with your fingertips.

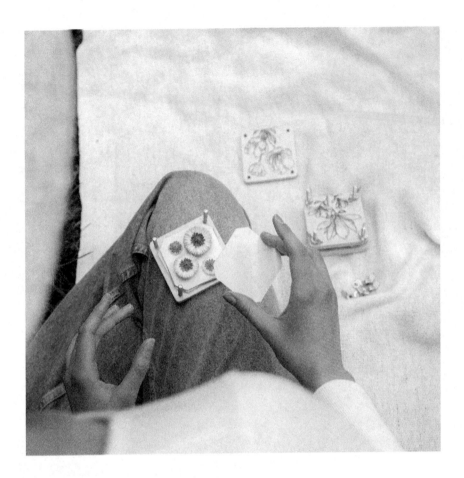

STEP 3 PRESSING TIME

Next, you will need to cover the flowers with another piece of paper. You can use the same type of paper that you used before or a different one. Gently press down on the flowers.

Then, place the flowers and paper between the pages of a heavy book or in a <u>flower press</u>. If you don't have a flower press, you can use any heavy object like a stack of books or a pan filled with cans (yep, that's how I started :-)).

STEP 4 WAITING TIME

The time it takes for flowers to press can vary depending on the type of flower and the humidity levels. Typically, it takes about two to three weeks for flowers to press fully. During this time, you will need to check on the flowers and change the paper if it becomes damp.

WHAT'S NEXT?

Once the flowers are fully pressed, you can remove them from the book or press. At this point, you can either leave them as is or add a coat of clear varnish to protect them. If you want to use them in an art or craft project, you can glue them to a piece of paper or use them to decorate a picture frame. My favorite glue is Mod Podge.

STORAGE

It is important to keep the pressed flowers in a dry and cool place to ensure they last as long as possible. You can also use a desiccant like silica gel to help absorb moisture and keep the flowers dry.

SUMMARY

Flower pressing is a fun and easy way to preserve the beauty of flowers. With a little patience and care, you can enjoy the beauty of your pressed flowers for years to come. Whether you're using them for art and craft projects or just want to keep them as a beautiful memory, flower pressing is a great way to enjoy the beauty of flowers for a long time.

In conclusion, pressing flowers is a great way to preserve the beauty of flowers for a long time. It is a simple process that requires only a few materials, but with a little patience, it will yield beautiful results. Remember to choose freshly picked flowers, prepare them properly, press them between a heavy book or flower press, and store them in a dry and cool place.

THE BEST PAPER TO HELP YOU PRESS FLOWERS

"Flowers always make people better, happier, and more helpful; they are sunshine, food and medicine for the soul." - Luther Burbank

*W*hat is blotter paper (also called blotting paper)? Is there a difference between blotting paper for the face and blotting paper for flowers?

Blotting paper for the face and blotting paper for flower pressing are similar in that they are both types of absorbent paper that are used to remove excess moisture and oil. However, there are also some key differences between the two.

Blotting paper for the face is specifically designed to be used on the skin. It is made of a lightweight paper infused with a powdery substance, usually rice or talc powder, that helps to absorb excess oil and shine on the skin. It is convenient and can be used on the go when you don't have access to a mirror. It gives a quick and refreshing touch-up.

On the other hand, <u>blotting paper for flower pressing</u> is designed to be used on flowers. It is made of a variety of materials, including cellulose, cotton, and linen, and is developed to be highly absorbent to remove excess moisture from flowers and preserve their shape, color, and detail. This is achieved by sandwiching the flowers between layers of blotting paper and applying pressure to squeeze out the excess moisture. It's ideal for craft projects, art, or display.

While both types of blotting paper serve similar purposes, they are designed for different uses and, therefore, have different properties. When looking for blotting paper, be sure to choose the right one for the task you have in mind, whether it's for your face or your flowers.

When you press flowers using blotting paper, the moisture is drawn out of the flowers and into the paper. The improved absorbency of blotting paper also helps to capture and retain the flowers' details.

As mentioned above, one of the key advantages of using blotting paper for flower pressing is its absorbency. By removing excess moisture from the flowers, blotting paper allows them to dry more quickly and retain their shape and color. This can be especially useful if you are working with flowers prone to wilting or with high water content.

WARNING

It is important to note that not all papers advertised as blotting paper for flower pressing are true blotting papers. In fact, many papers on the market that claim to be "blotting paper" are not absorbent enough to effectively remove moisture from flowers and preserve them properly.

When selecting blotting paper for flower pressing, be careful and make sure you are using a high-quality, absorbent paper specifically designed for this purpose. Avoid buying cheap paper labeled as "blotting paper" without doing proper research. It may not have the characteristics needed for flower pressing.

It is best to purchase blotting paper from reputable art or craft suppliers or by looking for reviews and feedback from other flower pressers to ensure you are getting a true blotting paper that will give you the best results for your flower pressing projects.

BLOTTING PAPER VS. PRINTING PAPER VS. WAX PAPER VS. PARCHMENT PAPER VS JAPANESE PAPER (WASHI) VS PAPER TOWEL

Each type of paper has its unique advantages and disadvantages, so it's important to understand the differences and choose the right paper for your project.

Printing paper

Standard printing paper is another option for flower pressing. It is widely available and is an affordable alternative to blotting paper. Standard printing paper is also acid-free, which means it will not turn yellow or damage the flowers over time.

A key disadvantage of using standard printing paper is that it is not as absorbent as blotting paper, so it may not remove as much moisture from the flowers. This increases the chances of your blooms becoming moldy. Additionally, standard printing paper is not as thick and durable as blotting paper, so once the paper has been used, you can't really reuse it for another batch of flowers.

Wax paper

Wax paper is another option for flower pressing. It is widely available and affordable. Wax paper is thin paper coated with a narrow layer of wax, which makes it moisture-resistant. This can help protect the flowers from humidity, dust, and other environmental factors.

A key disadvantage of using wax paper is that it is not absorbent, so it will not remove or soak up moisture from the flowers. Additionally, the wax coating can sometimes stick to the flowers, which can make it difficult to remove them from the paper once they are pressed. I would not recommend using wax paper to press flowers; it's best just to use it to protect your pressed blooms.

Parchment paper

Another option to consider when pressing flowers is parchment paper. Parchment paper is like wax paper in that it is moisture resistant, but it is also heat resistant and oven safe. This makes it a great option for pressing flowers using heat, like when using an iron or a microwave.

Parchment paper also provides a barrier between the flowers and any surface they are pressed on, which can prevent ink or other stains from transferring onto the flowers. Additionally, it is widely available and affordable. However, it is also not as absorbent as blotting paper, so it may not remove as much moisture from the flowers.

Japanese paper (Washi)

Our next option for pressing flowers is Japanese paper, also known as washi. Washi is a traditional Japanese paper made from the inner bark of the paper mulberry tree. It is known for its strength, durability, and beauty. It is also acid- and lignin-free, which means it will not yellow or damage the flowers over time.

However, it is not as absorbent as blotting paper, so it may not remove as much moisture from the flowers. Additionally, it is not as widely available and can be relatively expensive compared to other options.

Paper Kitchen Towel

Did you know that kitchen towels can be used as pressing tools? These handy little things are absorbent and inexpensive, and you probably already have some at home!

But here's the thing, they often have a cute little flower design on them which can leave a visible imprint on your pressed flowers. However, don't let that stop you. If you're using them for personal use, it might add a cute touch. This is just something to keep in mind if you're planning to use your pressed flowers for decorative purposes.

SUMMARY

While there are several types of paper that can be used for flower pressing, including parchment paper, printing paper, wax paper, Japanese paper, and paper towel, each has its unique advantages and disadvantages for flower pressing. However, blotting paper is the best option for removing excess moisture from flowers and preserving their color, shape, and detail.

In conclusion, if you are looking for a paper that will help you preserve flowers, blotting paper for flower pressing is the way to go. Its absorbent properties will help you dry your flowers quickly, retain their shape and color, and maintain their details. It is cost-effective, reusable, and lightweight, making it an excellent choice for flower pressing. No matter if you're a professional or just a beginner, blotting paper will help you create beautiful, unique flower art that you'll admire for years to come.

HOW LONG DOES IT TAKE TO PRESS FLOWERS?

"We are all dreaming of some magical rose garden over the horizon instead of enjoying the roses blooming outside our windows today." - Dale Carnegie

*W*hen it comes to flower pressing, one of the most common questions is, "How long does it take for flowers to press?" The answer depends on several factors, such as the type of flower, the humidity levels, and the method of pressing you use.

In this chapter, we will explore some of the factors that can affect the pressing time and give you an idea of what to expect.

TYPE OF FLOWER

First, let's talk about the type of flower. Some flowers press more quickly than others. For example, flowers with thinner petals and lower moisture, like pansies or violets, press more quickly than flowers with thicker petals and higher moisture, like roses or daisies. In general, delicate flowers press faster than larger, more robust flowers.

HUMIDITY LEVEL

Another factor that can affect the pressing time is the humidity level. High humidity can slow down the pressing process because it can cause the flowers to retain more moisture. This means that if you're pressing flowers in a location with high humidity, it may take longer for them to press than if you were pressing them in a location with low humidity.

PRESSING METHOD

The method of pressing also plays a role in the pressing time. If you're using a traditional flower press (i.e., <u>a wooden</u>

flower press), it can take anywhere from two to four weeks for flowers to press fully. However, if you're using a more modern method, such as a microwave press, the pressing time can be significantly shorter, taking only a few minutes.

It's important to keep in mind that the pressing time can vary depending on the type of flower, humidity levels, and the method of pressing. The best way to know when your flowers are fully pressed is to check on them periodically and see if they are flattened and dry. The drying process can take from two to three weeks, but it can take more or less time, depending on the circumstances.

WHOLE BLOOMS VS. SINGLE PETALS

When you press a whole flower, the petals and layers of the flower have to be separated, dried, and flattened evenly, which can take a lot of time and effort. However, when you press each petal separately, the process is much faster. The petals are already separated, so you don't have to worry about separating them yourself (plus, they're already being pressed and in contact with blotting paper).

Pressing flowers petal by petal may sound like a tedious task, but it can actually save you time, in the long run. Pressing whole flowers may seem like the quicker option, but at the same time it can take weeks for the flowers to fully dry and flatten out.

On the other hand, pressing petals individually can take a bit more time upfront, but the end result is usually worth it as the petals will be flattened and ready to use in a matter of days (this holds true for quite a few flowers, but not all). Plus, pressing petals separately allows for more control over the final product and can give a more delicate and intricate look to your pressed flowers.

If you're short on time or want to get your pressed flowers done quickly, pressing each petal individually is the way to go! So, don't be afraid to take the time to press your flowers petal by petal – it may just be the secret to beautiful, vibrant pressed flowers in a fraction of the time.

LITTLE RUB DOWN

One thing you can do to speed up the pressing process is to remove as much moisture from the flowers as possible before you press them. This can be done by gently patting them dry with a paper towel or allowing them to air dry for a few hours (before they start wilting).

This will help to reduce the amount of moisture that needs to be removed during the pressing process, thus shortening the pressing time.

If they are already dry on the surface, you can start pressing your blooms right away (the sooner they're being pressed, the better).

DRYING HACK

Another way to speed up the pressing process is to use a desiccant like silica gel. These are small packets filled with a moisture-absorbing material that can be placed inside the press with the flowers. However, the best type is very fine silica gel (powder) as that does not leave imprints on your blooms (it can get a bit dusty, though).

Simply sprinkle some powder over the paper (not the flowers to avoid imprints). The silica gel can help to absorb any remaining moisture in the flowers, speed up the drying process, and further reduce the risk of losing your blooms to nasty mold.

SUMMARY

In conclusion, the pressing time for flowers varies depending on several factors, including the type of flower, humidity levels, and the pressing method. In general, delicate flowers (for example, single petaled) will press faster than larger, more robust flowers. The humidity level can also affect the pressing time, and the method of pressing plays an important role too.

Pressing flowers whole can take anywhere from two to four weeks, depending on the type and size of the flower. Pressing flowers petal by petal, on the other hand, can take as little as a few days. This is because the pressure is applied directly to each individual petal, allowing for quicker and more thorough drying.

The best way to know when your flowers are fully pressed is to check on them periodically, and if you want to speed up the process, you can remove as much moisture from the flowers as possible and use a desiccant like silica gel.

PRESSING FLOWERS IN A BOOK

"After women, flowers are the most divine creations." - Christian Dior

*P*ressing flowers is a great way to preserve their beauty and create unique decorations for your home. One of the most traditional and simple methods for pressing flowers is using a book. Using a book to press flowers is an easy and affordable way to preserve your flowers, and it's perfect for those who want to press a few flowers at a time.

In this chapter, we will go over the steps for pressing flowers in a book and the materials you will need. We will also discuss the best types of flowers to press in a book and how to avoid common mistakes.

TO PRESS FLOWERS IN A BOOK, YOU WILL NEED THE FOLLOWING MATERIALS:

- Freshly picked flowers
- Printing paper or blotting paper
- A heavy book (like a dictionary or one that you don't need for now)
- A weight (like a brick or large can of food)

Step 1: Gather your flowers and prepare them for pressing.

Choose flowers that are freshly picked and in good condition. Avoid using flowers that are wilted or have brown edges, as they will not give good results. Some popular flowers that press well in a book include violets, pansies, and daisies. These flowers have thin petals and are more suited for pressing in a book than thick-petaled flowers like roses.

Step 2: Lay the flowers out on a piece of printing paper or, ideally, blotting paper.

This is to protect your blooms and add extra absorbent sheets to soak up the moisture from the flowers. Gently spread the flowers out so that they do not overlap. It's also good to flatten the blooms with your fingertips.

NB. Here is the chapter on <u>The best paper to help you press flowers</u>.

Step 3: Cover the flowers with another piece of paper.

Once your flowers are sandwiched between two sheets of paper, gently press down.

Step 4: Carefully place the flowers and paper between the pages of a heavy book.

Make sure the book is thick and heavy, as a thinner book will not provide enough pressure to press the flowers effectively.

Step 5: Place a weight on top of the book to add extra pressure on the flowers.

This step helps make sure all parts of your blooms are in contact with the paper. The moisture gets released from the blooms and is quickly soaked up by the paper.

Step 6: Leave the flowers to press for two to three weeks.

Check on the flowers while they are pressing and change the paper if it becomes damp.

Some flowers will press better than others in a book. Flowers with thin petals, like pansies and violets, will press better than thick-petaled flowers like roses. If you want to press thick-petaled flowers, it's best to press each petal and layer separately to ensure all parts of the flower are pressed evenly.

TYPE OF BOOK

Another important thing to note is that some books are better suited for pressing flowers than others. Avoid using books with soft covers as they don't exert enough pressure throughout the whole flower. Also, if your book does not close when you place your blooms inside it, the flower may be too thick and/ or the book too small. In this case, only a part of it will get pressed, and the other part will just air dry, then get crushed or go moldy. If that is the case, choose a bigger book or press parts of the flowers separately, then re-assemble them once pressed and ready.

To be honest, the best technique for pressing thick and whole flowers in a book is by pressing them petal by petal to ensure great results. Consider this method if your flower has more than two layers of petals.

BOOK CARE

Be aware that pressing flowers in a book can be risky for the book itself, as the moisture from the flowers can damage the pages. To avoid this, you can place the flowers and paper between wax paper or parchment paper before placing them in the book. However, if you don't mind risking damaging your book, feel free to pop your flowers straight inside (as mentioned before, this is best for small, single-petaled blooms).

Additionally, the ink from the pages of the book can sometimes transfer onto the pressed flowers, which can be a problem if you want to use the flowers for decorative purposes. To avoid this, place the flowers and paper between wax paper or parchment paper before placing them in the book. This will act as a barrier between the flowers and the pages of the book, preventing any ink transfer.

Another alternative is to use a clean, unused notebook with a hard cover, i.e., one that doesn't have any ink, then just put another book on top of it. However, if you want to jump into flower pressing like a pro and don't want to risk your precious books, then definitely consider using a wooden flower press specifically made for the purpose.

SUMMARY

In conclusion, pressing flowers in a book is a traditional and easy way to preserve their beauty. However, it's important to choose the right type of flowers and the right book to ensure the flowers press well. Flowers with thin petals, like pansies and violets, are better suited for pressing in a book than whole, thick-petaled flowers like garden roses. Additionally, it's important to protect the flowers from dust and moisture and prevent ink transfer by using wax paper or parchment paper.

PRESSING A ROSE PETAL BY PETAL

"If we could see the miracle of a single flower clearly, our whole life would change." - Buddha

*I*f you're like me, you probably have a few rose bushes and maybe even a branch or two of lavender. If you want to preserve the beauty of these flowers for years to come, it's time for some serious flower pressing!

No matter what kind of flower you're after or whether the flowers are on their way out, this guide is going to show you how to press them so that they last longer than just an hour in water. So, pull up a chair by your favorite watering can, and let's get started.

With a little bit of patience and the right supplies, you can turn your fresh roses into long-lasting pressed flowers that you can use in all sorts of crafts and decorations.

WILD ROSES OR GARDEN ROSES?

When it comes to pressing roses, it doesn't matter whether you're working with wild or garden varieties. That's because we're pressing the petals one by one rather than the whole flower.

However, if you were to press whole roses, you might find that wild roses are easier to work with because they tend to have fewer petals and be smaller, which means there's less surface area, and it's easier to make them flatter. So, whether you're working with wild or garden roses, you can rest assured that the process of pressing the petals individually will be relatively the same.

Images: Wild rose vs. garden rose

HERE'S A STEP-BY-STEP GUIDE TO HELP YOU GET STARTED:

Choose your roses

Once you've decided to press roses, it's time to pick which ones. Choose roses that are fully opened and not damaged. You want a variety of colors and sizes so your rose-pressing experience is as enjoyable as possible.

Don't choose any damaged flowers because those can ruin the whole process by getting moldy during pressing. Flower pressing magnifies any blemishes or imperfections, so choose your blooms carefully.

Get your supplies together

You'll need a few things for this process. First and foremost is a <u>flower press</u>. Look for a traditional wooden flower press with bolts and nuts, as this will make it easier to adjust the pressure on your blooms.

You'll also want some paper towel to remove excess water from the petals and <u>blotting paper</u> for the pressing process.

Prepare your roses

To begin, remove any foliage from your roses. This can be very therapeutic as you have to be focused to avoid ripping the leaves or petals.

Next, remove each petal individually by holding it between two fingers at its base and gently pulling up on it until it separates from the stem. Don't worry if some tear apart; that's fine, but don't use them! We are going to press many petals to ensure we have a good collection.

Once all the petals are removed from their stems or roots, arrange them all on a paper towel. Then, gently dab your individual petals with another paper towel sheet to remove any excess water. Once the petals are dry, you can begin pressing.

This is the most fun part because it's so easy and enjoyable.

Press the flowers

- ▶ Place each petal on the blotting paper individually so they don't touch one another.
- ▶ Close the press and check it about five days later. If there's still moisture on the blotting paper, change it out for a new

sheet of blotting paper.

- ▶ If you don't have a flower press, use a heavy book or stack of magazines instead.
- ▶ Individual rose petals press a lot quicker than whole roses, and the chances of mold are a lot less. It may take about two weeks to get your petals dry, pressed, and ready for your creations.

Cleaning up and storing pressed roses

After pressing, store your pressed rose petals in a cool, dry place. While it's tempting to leave them out on display all day and get ready for the next party or event, don't do this! Store them away from direct sunlight and high humidity levels. If possible, put them in airtight containers with some silica gel sprinkled inside (to keep your petals perfectly dry) until you're ready to create.

SUMMARY

Pressed flowers are a great way to preserve the beauty of your roses, and they're even better when you make them yourself. Once all your petals are ready, you can reconstruct these perfect flowers in any way you like. Don't forget to add the foliage you pressed, as this will make your rose art pieces even more natural and real.

With this simple process, you can turn your fresh roses into stunning, long-lasting pressed beauties that you can use in all sorts of crafts and decorations.

WOODEN VS. MICROWAVABLE FLOWER PRESSES

"A rose can never be a sunflower, and a sunflower can never be a rose. All flowers are beautiful in their own way, and that's like women too." - Miranda Kerr

*W*hen it comes to pressing flowers, there are two main types of flower presses to choose from: wooden flower presses and microwavable flower presses. Both have their own unique characteristics and advantages, and it can be difficult to decide which one to use. In this chapter, we will compare the two types of flower presses and help you decide which one is best for your needs.

WOODEN FLOWER PRESS

A <u>wooden flower press</u> is a traditional type of press that has been used for centuries to preserve flowers. It typically consists of two wooden boards and several layers of paper or cloth. The flowers are placed between the layers and then clamped together with the boards to apply pressure.

Wooden flower presses can be adjusted to fit any size of flower, and they are easy to use. With the aid of wing nuts, you also have much better control over the pressure when pressing your blooms. They are also a traditional way of preserving flowers and can become a nice decorative piece in your home.

A key advantage of using a wooden flower press is that it is a natural and eco-friendly option. Wooden presses are made from sustainable materials, and they don't require any electricity to operate (or a microwave). Additionally, wooden presses are durable and can be used for many years, making them a great investment.

On the downside, using a wooden flower press can make it take a long time to press flowers, usually two to three weeks. Because of that time, you may need more than one press if you want to press many blooms at once.

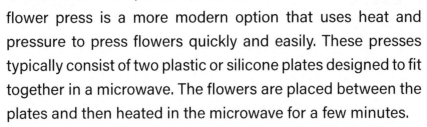

MICROWAVABLE FLOWER PRESS

On the other hand, a microwavable flower press is a more modern option that uses heat and pressure to press flowers quickly and easily. These presses typically consist of two plastic or silicone plates designed to fit together in a microwave. The flowers are placed between the plates and then heated in the microwave for a few minutes.

Typically, it takes about two or three minutes for flowers to press fully. During this time, you will need to check on the flowers and change the paper if it becomes damp. The best way is to use 15-second bursts of heat to reduce the risk of burning. However, it will still depend on the blooms you're pressing in a microwave.

As you can see, a key advantage of using a microwavable flower press is that it is fast and convenient. You can press a batch of flowers in a matter of minutes, whereas traditional methods can take weeks. Additionally, microwavable presses are smaller and more compact, making them easy to store.

On the downside, microwavable flower presses can handle your blooms a lot less delicately than traditional methods. There is a higher risk of over-drying or even burning the flowers if you are not careful with the time

and temperature. Additionally, not all flowers are suitable for pressing in a microwave, and some flowers may not press as well in a microwave as they would with traditional methods.

THE VERDICT

In conclusion, both wooden flower presses and microwavable flower presses have their unique characteristics and advantages. Wooden flower presses are natural and eco-friendly, while microwavable flower presses are fast and convenient.

If you are looking for a traditional and sustainable option, a wooden press might be the best choice, but if you need a quick and easy way to press flowers, a microwavable press might be a better option. Ultimately, the choice depends on your personal preference and the type of flowers you want to press.

Remember, pressing flowers is not only about speed but also about the care and patience you put into it. Happy flower pressing!

ACHIEVING A BUG-FREE PRESSED FLOWER MASTERPIECE

"The flower that follows the sun does so even in cloudy days." - Robert Leighton

$\mathcal{D}$o you hold your breath each time you unveil a pressed flower, fearing the sight of a tiny uninvited guest? Tiny bugs in the intricately pressed flowers are an unexpected, unsightly challenge, capable of turning our preservation endeavors into painstaking efforts.

Let's explore ways to ensure our flowers remain as captivating in their frames as they were in their natural bloom, undisturbed by these miniature intruders.

PRE-PRESSING RITUALS

Choosing flowers – the foundation of art: Handpicking each flower sets the foundation for your artwork. Look for the healthiest flowers that are radiant in their bloom. Any signs of bugs? A little damage, perhaps? It's a no-go. This preemptive decision has a significant say in the outcome of your art.

Eagle-eyed inspection: Inspect. Every. Single. Flower. Bring out the magnifying glass and check for signs of minuscule invaders, their eggs, or their larvae. They can be crafty, hiding beneath the petals and leaves. A well-conducted investigation can save the artwork from potential damage.

A gentle brush-off: Time for a gentle cleaning session. Equip yourself with a soft paintbrush and brush the surfaces lightly. Who knows, you might send a few lingering insects packing.

Flower bubble bath: A lukewarm bath with a dash of dish soap can do wonders. Dunk the flowers for about a quarter of an hour. This acts as a non-harmful yet effective insect eviction notice. After their bath, give them a rinse, followed by a soft towel patting.

Air-drying: Thorough drying is crucial because you can't risk mold growth, which, by the way, bugs love. A hairdryer on a gentle setting can help, or let the air work its magic in a well-ventilated spot.

POST PRESSING AND FRAMING – SAFEGUARDING ART

Proper storage – A key step: Your framed artwork is like a newly hatched bird. It needs proper care. Store it in a cool, dry environment. Humidity can be an open invitation for bugs and mold.

Regular check-ups: Treat your artwork like a prized possession. Regularly check for signs of bugs by looking for tiny holes or discoloration. If you find any, you know what to do.

Sealing the masterpiece: Think of acid-free tape as your knight in shining armor, protecting your artwork from bugs. Make sure no crevices remain for bugs to sneak in.

The herbal guardian: Herbs like lavender and mint can be your fragrant allies. Placing sachets of these near your stored pressed flowers not only adds a refreshing aroma but also helps in keeping bugs at bay before creating your frames.

Insecticides – the last resort: Severe infestations may require the use of insecticides. Just be sure to apply them cautiously. We wouldn't want them to touch the flowers, right?

With these steps in your artist's arsenal, you can create, knowing your artwork is protected. A bit of time spent on the pre-pressing rituals and some post-framing strategies, and you're all set to create an enduring, bug-free masterpiece.

HOW TO PRESERVE PRESSED FLOWERS

"Flowers... are a proud assertion that a ray of beauty out-values all the utilities of the world." - Ralph Waldo Emerson

*P*ressing flowers is a great way to preserve the beauty of flowers for a long time, but it's not the only step in keeping them looking beautiful. Once your flowers are fully pressed, you'll need to take some steps to preserve them so that they will last as long as possible.

In this chapter, we will go over some tips and techniques for preserving your pressed flowers, including their color.

COMPLETELY DRY

The first step in preserving pressed flowers is to make sure they are completely dry. If your flowers are still damp when you remove them from the press, they will continue to dry and may warp or become discolored.

To ensure your flowers dry out fully, place them in a dry place that has good air ventilation.

PROTECT FROM THE ELEMENTS

Once your flowers are dry, you'll want to protect them from dust, light, and moisture. You can place them between the pages of a book or in an airtight container. You can also use a clear varnish to protect the flowers and give them a shiny or matt finish (I prefer the latter). Applying a coat of varnish will not only protect the flowers from dust and light but also enhance their color and keep them looking fresh.

USE SILICA GEL

Another way to preserve your pressed flowers is to use a desiccant like silica gel. These are small packets filled with moisture-absorbing material that can be placed inside the container or book with the flowers. They can help to absorb any remaining moisture in the flowers and keep them dry.

If you keep your pressed blooms inside airtight containers, just sprinkle some silica gel at the bottom of each container. This way, if any moisture manages to get through, it will be quickly soaked up by the gel, keeping your blooms nice and dry.

DISPLAY

If you want to display your pressed flowers, you can frame them or use them to decorate a picture frame. To do this, you'll need to glue the flowers to a piece of paper or cardstock using a glue stick or craft glue. Once they are securely attached, you can place them in a frame or use them to decorate a picture frame. Alternatively, there are gorgeous floating frames out there that will also offer some protection to your blooms.

You can also use pressed flowers to create art and craft projects. For example, creating a pressed flower wall hanging or decorating a piece of jewelry. The possibilities are endless!

SIDE NOTE

It's also important to note that some flowers will preserve better than others. Flowers with thin petals, such as pansies and violets, will preserve better than flowers with thick petals, such as roses or daisies. Additionally, flowers that are pressed at the peak of their bloom will often preserve better than those that are pressed past their prime.

PRESERVING THE COLOR OF YOUR FLOWERS

Preserving the color of pressed flowers is an art that requires a bit of patience and some special techniques. While it's not possible to retain the vibrant hues of freshly picked flowers, it is possible to preserve the color of pressed flowers for a longer period.

Here are some tips on how to preserve the color of pressed flowers:

CHOOSE THE RIGHT FLOWERS

Choosing the right flowers can have a big impact on how well they preserve their color when pressed. Some flowers are more likely to retain their color when pressed than others. Flowers with thin petals, such as daisies and violets, tend to preserve their color well. Flowers with thick petals, such as roses and peonies, may also preserve their color well.

On the other hand, flowers with white or pale petals tend to fade quickly when pressed, as the pigments that give them their color are not as concentrated. Additionally, flowers with bright or vibrant colors may fade more quickly than those with more subdued colors.

PRESS THE FLOWERS AT THE RIGHT TIME

Pressing flowers at the right time of their growth can help to preserve their color because the flowers will be at their peak of bloom. When flowers are at their peak of bloom, they contain the highest concentration of pigments, which are the substances that give flowers their color. By pressing the flowers at this stage, you can help to preserve as much of their color as possible.

In contrast, if you press flowers that are past their peak of bloom, they will have already begun to fade and will not retain their color as well. Additionally, if you press wilted or damaged flowers, they will not retain their color well because the pigments in the petals may already have been damaged.

USE A FLOWER PRESS

Traditional <u>flower presses</u> work great because they give you more control over how much pressure gets applied to the flowers each time. It's definitely worth investing in a flower press if you are thinking of pressing blooms more regularly.

The most important thing here is making sure your arrangements stay dry over time until they're ready for display!

USE BLOTTING PAPER

Blotting paper can help to preserve the color of pressed flowers by absorbing excess moisture from the flowers as they dry. When flowers are pressed, they release moisture that can cause the colors to fade or become discolored.

By using blotting paper, you can remove some of this excess moisture, helping to preserve the color of the flowers.

AVOID EXPOSING THE FLOWERS TO DIRECT LIGHT

Direct sunlight can cause pressed flowers to fade and change color because it can damage the pigments in the petals. Pigments are the substances in flowers that give them their color. They are sensitive to light, heat, and other environmental factors. When exposed to direct sunlight, the pigments in the petals can break down, causing the flowers to fade or change color.

In addition to fading, direct sunlight can also cause pressed flowers to become discolored. This can happen because the heat from the sun can cause the pigments to shift, resulting in a change in the overall color of the flowers.

USE A FIXATIVE

A fixative is a chemical that helps to preserve the color of pressed flowers. There are several types of fixatives available, including hair spray and polyvinyl acetate (PVA). These fixatives work by creating a protective barrier over the flowers, which helps to preserve their color.

To use a fixative, simply spray the fixative over the pressed flowers. The fixative will create a thin film over the flowers, helping to protect them from light, heat, and other environmental factors. This will help to preserve their color for a longer period.

Be careful not to use too much as the dry flowers can easily curl up from the excess moisture, so a thin mist will work better.

STORE THE FLOWERS CORRECTLY

Proper storage is key to preserving the color of pressed flowers. Avoid storing the flowers in a damp or humid place, as this can cause them to become moldy. Instead, store the flowers in an airtight container (with a sprinkle of fine silica gel to keep them dry) or frame them under glass to protect them from the elements.

SUMMARY

Preserving pressed flowers is an important step in keeping them looking beautiful for a long time. To preserve pressed flowers, make sure they are completely dry, protect them from dust, light, and moisture, and use a desiccant like silica gel. You can also display your pressed flowers by framing them or using them to decorate a picture frame, or even create art and craft projects.

Several techniques can be used to preserve the color of pressed flowers. These techniques include choosing the right flowers, pressing the flowers at the right time, using a flower press, avoiding exposing the flowers to light, using a fixative, and storing the flowers correctly.

By following these tips, you can help to preserve the color of pressed flowers for a longer period. While it may not be possible to keep the vibrant colors of all your blooms, you can still enjoy the beauty of pressed flowers for months or even years to come.

Overall, preserving the color of pressed flowers is an art that requires a bit of patience and some special techniques. With the right tools and techniques, you can create beautiful, long-lasting pressed flower arrangements that add natural beauty to any space.

SEALING PRESSED FLOWERS TO PROTECT THEM

If you tend to a flower, it will bloom, no matter how many weeds surround it." - Matshona Dhliwayo

*P*ressed flowers are a beautiful and delicate way to preserve the natural beauty of flowers. However, without proper care, the colors and shapes of the flowers can fade over time. Sealing pressed flowers is a way to help preserve their color and shape and can also help to protect them from damage or fading caused by light and air exposure.

COLOR PRESERVATION

There are several benefits to sealing pressed flowers. The most obvious is that it helps to preserve the color of the flowers. Without sealing, the colors of the flowers can fade or change over time, especially if they are exposed to light or air. Sealing the flowers helps to lock in the color and prevent fading so the flowers will look as beautiful as they did when they were first pressed.

PROTECTION

Another benefit of sealing pressed flowers is that it helps to protect them from damage. Pressed flowers are delicate and can be easily damaged if they are handled or transported improperly. Sealing the flowers can help reinforce their structure and make them more damage-resistant.

There are several reasons why people may choose to seal their pressed flowers. Some people may simply want to preserve the natural beauty of the flowers for as long as possible. Others may want to use the flowers for crafts or art projects, and sealing the flowers can help to ensure that they remain in good condition throughout the project.

WHAT ARE THE BEST PRODUCTS FOR SEALING?

Several different products can be used to seal pressed flowers, and each has its pros and cons. Some common options include the following:

Clear nail polish

This is a quick and easy option for sealing pressed flowers, and it is widely available at most stores. Simply brush a thin layer of clear nail polish over the flowers to seal them. The main advantage of using clear nail polish is that it is inexpensive and easy to find. However, it may not be as effective at preserving the color of the flowers as some other options, and it can also be prone to chipping or flaking over time.

Acrylic spray

This is another popular option for sealing pressed flowers. Simply spray a thin layer of acrylic over the flowers to seal them. Acrylic spray is more durable than clear nail polish, and it can help to preserve the color of the flowers more effectively. However, it may be more expensive and harder to find than clear nail polish.

Archival-quality sealant

This is a more expensive option, but it is the most effective at preserving the color and condition of pressed flowers. Archival-quality sealants are specifically designed to be long-lasting and resistant to fading or damage. However, they may be harder to find and more expensive than other options.

Mod Podge

One of the best options for sealing pressed flowers is Mod Podge, which is a clear, water-based glue that is specifically designed for use in crafts and art projects. Mod Podge can be used to seal pressed flowers, as well as a wide variety of other materials, and it dries to a clear, matte finish. It is easy to apply and dries quickly, and it is also very durable, making it an excellent choice for preserving pressed flowers.

Follow the below steps to seal pressed flowers:

1. Press the flowers using a flower press or between the pages of a heavy book. Allow the flowers to dry completely, which can take several days to a week, depending on the type of flower and the humidity.
2. Once the flowers are dry, carefully arrange them on a sheet of blotting paper or other flat surface.
3. Using a brush or spray, apply a thin layer of sealant over the flowers. Make sure to cover the entire surface of the flowers, but be careful not to apply too much

sealant, as it can cause the flowers to become stiff or discolored. Also, if you apply too much of it, the very thin petals can curl up from contact with a lot of moisture.

4. Allow the sealant to dry completely, which may take several hours or overnight, depending on the product being used.

5. Once the sealant is dry, the flowers are ready to be displayed or used in crafts or art projects.

In summary, pressed flowers are a beautiful and delicate way to capture the natural beauty of flowers, but without proper care, their colors and shapes can fade over time. That's where sealing comes in!

Sealing pressed flowers helps to preserve their color and shape and can also protect them from damage or fading caused by light and air exposure. There are several products that can be used to seal pressed flowers, each with its own pros and cons. Clear nail polish is a quick and easy option, but it may not be as effective at preserving color. Acrylic spray is more durable, but it may be harder to find and more expensive. Archival-quality sealant is the most effective at preserving color and condition, but it is also the most expensive. However, our favorite one to use is a clear-drying craft glue which is great value for money and is widely available – Mod Podge.

No matter which product you choose, be sure to follow the manufacturer's instructions carefully and allow the sealant to dry completely before displaying or handling your beautiful, pressed flowers.

PRESSED FLOWERS AND ARTIFICIAL COLOR ENHANCEMENT

"The flower doesn't dream of the bee, it blossoms and the bee comes." - Mark Nepo

*A*re you looking for a way to take your flower preservation art to the next level?

One of the very interesting aspects of flower preservation is the opportunity to enhance the colors of pressed flowers. By using different techniques and materials, you can create stunning and vibrant floral displays. But with so many options available, it can be hard to know where to start.

In this chapter, we'll take a closer look at the art of color-enhancing pressed flowers and share tips and techniques for achieving beautiful and long-lasting results.

Whether you're a beginner or an experienced flower preservation artist, you'll find lots of useful information that I gathered over the years of pressing various blooms. So, let's dive in and explore the exciting world of color-enhanced pressed flowers!

When you press flowers, you may notice that the colors change, turn brown, or fade over time. This is because the pigments and chemicals responsible for the vibrant colors in flowers are sensitive to various factors, such as heat, air, and light.

Here is some more in-depth info about why flowers fade or change color.

ULTRAVIOLET (UV) LIGHT EXPOSURE:

When flowers are exposed to sunlight, they undergo a process called photodegradation. This process is caused by the breakdown of the pigments in the flower's petals, which causes them to change color and eventually fade. The pigments in flowers are sensitive to light, and when exposed to UV radiation from the sun, they start to break down and lose their color.

This is particularly true for flowers displayed near windows or in direct sunlight.

CHLOROPHYLL DEGRADATION:

Chlorophyll is the pigment responsible for the green color in leaves and stems. When flowers are pressed, the plant tissues break down, and the chlorophyll degrades, leading to a change in color or browning. That's why I always recommend gradually tightening the nuts in your flower press rather than going all out and accidentally crushing your precious blooms.

PRESSING PROCESS ITSELF:

In addition to photodegradation, the process of pressing flowers can also cause them to change color or fade. When flowers are pressed, the moisture inside them is removed, which can cause the petals to dry out and become brittle. This can lead to a loss of color and a change in the flower's texture.

By understanding the factors that contribute to color changes and fading in pressed flowers, we can take steps to preserve the beauty of our creations for longer.

All in all, when pressing flowers, it's best to accept that the color of the blooms you pressed will be different to their original shade. So, our goal is to minimize that change or perhaps bring back a bit more life to our pressed petals using various color enhancing methods.

Reducing the amount your pressed flowers fade:

1. Use a flower press that allows for even pressure distribution and proper ventilation.
2. Press flowers when they are fresh and at their peak, as older flowers may be more susceptible to fading and color changes.
3. Choose flowers with vibrant colors and high pigment content, as these may retain their color better when pressed.
4. Handle the flowers with care and avoid touching them too much, as this can cause the petals to break or lose their color.
5. Avoid exposing the pressed flowers to direct sunlight or other sources of UV radiation, as this can cause the pigments to break down and fade.
6. Store the pressed flowers in a cool, dry place that is free from direct sunlight or moisture.
7. Consider using a UV-resistant coating or spray to protect the pressed flowers from fading and discoloration over time.

8. Use high-quality materials and tools that are designed for flower pressing, as these may help to preserve the color and texture of the flowers.
9. Consider pressing petals individually, if possible, for better control, then reconstruct your bloom using the ones that preserved the best.

Techniques to enhance the color of your pressed blooms with dye:

- Watercolor paints: Artists can use watercolor paints to add color and depth to pressed flowers. This technique involves diluting the paint with water and applying it to the petals with a small brush. The artist can layer different colors to achieve the desired effect.
- Acrylic paints: Acrylic paints can also be used to enhance the colors of pressed flowers. The artist can mix different colors to create a custom shade and then apply the paint to the petals using a brush or sponge. Acrylic paints are known for their vibrant colors and durability.
- Alcohol inks: Alcohol inks are highly pigmented, fast-drying inks that can be used to enhance the colors of pressed flowers. The artist can apply the ink directly to the petals using a dropper or brush or use a spray bottle to create a more diffuse effect. Alcohol inks are known for their bright colors and ability to create unique patterns and textures.
- Food coloring: Food coloring can be used to enhance the colors of pressed flowers. The artist can mix

different colors to create a custom shade, and then apply the coloring to the petals using a dropper or brush. Food coloring is a simple and affordable option for color enhancement but may not be as durable as other techniques.

o Natural dyes: Some artists prefer to use natural dyes, such as beet juice or turmeric, to enhance the colors of pressed flowers. These dyes can be applied to the petals using a brush or dropper, creating unique and subtle shades. However, natural dyes may not be as long-lasting as other techniques and may require more experimentation to achieve the desired effect.

o Markers or pens: Fine-tip markers or pens with archival-quality ink can be used to outline or add details to the pressed flowers, enhancing their colors and overall appearance.

o Pigment powders: Artists can use pigment powders, such as mica or pearl-ex powders, to add a touch of shimmer or iridescence to the pressed flowers. These powders can be applied with a brush or mixed with a medium, like a clear varnish, and then applied to the flowers.

o Sealants or glazes: Applying a clear sealant or glaze, such as acrylic medium or Mod Podge, can help enhance and protect the colors of the pressed flowers.

Which method is the best?

It's difficult to say which technique is most used by flower preservation artists, as different artists may have their own preferred methods based on their personal style and the specific flowers they are working with. However, some techniques may be more popular than others, depending on the desired effect or level of difficulty.

As for which technique gives the best results with the lowest risk of failure, that can also depend on the artist's skill level and experience. Generally speaking, watercolor and acrylic paints are popular choices for color-enhancing pressed flowers because they are widely available, easy to use, and can produce vibrant and long-lasting colors. Alcohol inks can also be effective but may require more experimentation to achieve the desired effect and may be more difficult to control. Natural dyes and food coloring can be affordable and provide unique results, but they may not be as long-lasting or predictable as other techniques.

Ultimately, the best technique will depend on the artist's preferences, the specific flowers they are working with, and the desired effect. It's always a good idea to experiment with different materials and techniques to find what works best for your unique style and approach to flower preservation.

SUMMARY

In summary, flower preservation is the process of pressing and preserving flowers for decorative purposes. Flowers can change color and fade due to a variety of factors, including exposure to sunlight, moisture, and air. Flower preservation artists can use a variety of techniques to reduce fading and enhance the colors of pressed flowers, including using acid-free paper, applying a fixative spray, using UV-resistant glass frames, and storing flowers in a cool and dry place.

Some popular techniques for color-enhancing pressed flowers include using watercolor paints, acrylic paints, alcohol inks, natural dyes, and food coloring. Each technique has its advantages and disadvantages, and the best technique will depend on the artist's personal style and preferences, as well as the specific flowers they are working with.

Overall, flower preservation is a creative and rewarding hobby that allows artists to capture the beauty and essence of nature in their art. With proper techniques and materials, pressed flowers can be enjoyed for many years to come.

HOW TO MAKE DRIED FLOWER CONFETTI AT HOME

"A weed is but an unloved flower." - Ella Wheeler Wilcox

onfetti is a symbol of joy and celebration, adding a touch of magic to some of life's most special moments. Whether it's a wedding, a birthday, or another momentous occasion, using confetti is a simple yet powerful way to add a burst of color and happiness to the atmosphere. But what if you could elevate this simple joy even further by incorporating the beauty of nature into your confetti mix?

Dried flowers have the power to add a touch of romance, elegance, and whimsy to any event, and this chapter will guide you through the process of turning them into confetti that will be remembered for years to come.

From choosing the perfect flowers to drying them in the most effective way, we will explore the options available to you so that you can create confetti that perfectly captures the essence of your special moment.

Whether you want a confetti mix that is natural and organic or one that is delicate and romantic, this chapter will help you turn your vision into a reality.

FRESH FLOWERS VS. DRIED FLOWERS FOR CONFETTI

Using dried flowers for confetti is generally better than using fresh flowers for several reasons, as follows:

1. Longevity: Dried flowers can last for several months or even years, whereas fresh flowers will only last a few

days before wilting and becoming unsightly.

2. Convenience: Drying flowers takes time, but once they are dried, they can be stored and used as needed. Fresh flowers need to be purchased closer to the event and may not be available at the desired time.

3. Allergies: Fresh flowers can cause allergies in some people, especially those with hay fever or asthma. Dried flowers, on the other hand, are less likely to cause allergies.

4. Cost: Fresh flowers can be expensive, especially if they are out of season. Dried flowers can be less expensive, especially if you grow your own or buy them in bulk.

In summary, using dried flowers for confetti is the better option because of their longevity, convenience, reduced allergy risk, and cost-effectiveness.

WHOLE FLOWERS, SINGLE PETALS, OR CRUSHED BLOOMS?

The choice between using whole flowers, just petals, or crushed flowers as confetti depends on the desired look and feel of the event.

▶ Whole flowers can create a dramatic and elegant effect, especially if you choose larger blooms such as roses or hydrangeas (but do not throw these).

▶ Petals, on the other hand, are a great option if you want a more delicate and romantic feel, as they create a gentle shower of color.

▶ Crushed flowers can provide a more natural and organic look and can be a good choice if you want the confetti to blend in with the environment.

If you choose to use whole flowers as confetti, be aware that you will need a lot of them compared to using just petals or crushed flowers. Whole flowers take up more space and therefore, you will need more of them to achieve the desired look and coverage. This can be a factor to consider if you have limited space or budget.

In contrast, using petals or crushed flowers can be a more cost-effective option as they take up less space and can be produced in larger quantities with fewer flowers. It is important to consider these factors and plan accordingly when choosing between whole flowers, petals, or crushed flowers for your confetti.

BEST FLOWERS FOR CONFETTI?

The best flowers for making dried flower confetti are those that hold their color well after drying. Some popular choices include lavender, roses, hydrangea, baby's breath, statice, strawflowers, and daisies.

Flowers with a more delicate structure, such as petunias or carnations, may not hold up as well after drying and may not be the best choice for confetti. Consider choosing flowers that have bright, vibrant colors that will make a statement.

Additionally, consider choosing seasonal and readily available flowers to ensure you have access to them when you need them. Regardless of the type of flower you choose, be sure to dry them properly before your event using one of the methods mentioned earlier to ensure they will hold up well as confetti.

DRYING FLOWERS FOR CONFETTI

Fresh flowers can be dried using various methods to create colorful and long-lasting confetti. There are several drying methods to choose from, including silica gel, flower press, and books. Each method has its pros and cons, so it's important to choose the one that best fits your needs. In this chapter, we will discuss each method in detail and compare the pros and cons of each.

METHOD 1: SILICA GEL

Silica gel is a common drying agent that can be found in many stores. This method is fast and effective, making it the perfect choice for those who need dried flowers quickly. To dry flowers with silica gel, you will need a container, silica gel, and fresh flowers. Simply place the silica gel in the container, arrange the flowers on top, and seal the lid. The silica gel will absorb the moisture from the flowers and dry them in a few days.

Pros:

▸ Fast drying time: Flowers can be dried in as little as 24 hours.

- ▶ Effective: Silica gel is very effective in removing moisture from flowers, making it the perfect choice for those who need dried flowers quickly.
- ▶ Easy to use: Simply place the flowers in a container with silica gel, seal the lid, and wait for the flowers to dry.

Cons:

- ▶ Cost: Silica gel can be expensive, especially if you need a large amount.
- ▶ Messy: Silica gel can be messy to work with, as it is a fine powder that can easily get everywhere.
- ▶ Toxicity: Silica gel is not toxic, but it is not recommended for use around pets or children as it can cause irritation if inhaled.

METHOD 2: FLOWER PRESS

A flower press is another option for drying flowers. This method involves using a flower press, which, as described earlier, is a device that compresses flowers between two pieces of wood and a tightening mechanism. To dry flowers with a flower press, simply place the flowers between two pieces of cardboard, tighten the press, and leave it for several days. The pressure from the press will remove the moisture from the flowers, leaving them dry and flat.

Pros:

- ▶ Effective: Flower presses are highly effective in removing moisture from flowers, making them perfect for those who want their flowers to look as close to their original state as possible.

▸ Easy to use: Simply place the flowers in the press, tighten it, and wait for the flowers to dry.

▸ Long-lasting: Flowers dried with a flower press will maintain their color and shape for a long time, making them perfect for creating confetti.

Cons:

▸ Slow drying time: Flowers dried with a flower press can take several days or even weeks to dry completely.

▸ Cost: Flower presses can be expensive, especially if you need a large one.

▸ Limited size: Flower presses are limited in size, so you may need multiple presses if you have a large quantity of flowers to dry.

METHOD 3: BOOKS

The third method for drying flowers is using books. This method involves arranging the flowers between the pages of a book and leaving them for several days. The pressure from the book will remove the moisture from the flowers, leaving them dry and flat.

Pros:

▸ Easy to use: Simply place the flowers between the pages of a book and wait for them to dry.

- Cost-effective: This method is cost-effective as you likely already have books at home.
- Natural drying: The natural drying process of this method helps maintain the color and shape of the flowers.

Cons:

- Slow drying time: Flowers dried using books can take several days or even weeks to dry completely.
- Limited size: Books are limited in size, so you may need multiple books if you have a large quantity of flowers to dry.
- Bulky: Using books to dry flowers can take up a lot of space, especially if you have many books and flowers.
- Damage to books: The moisture from the flowers can damage the pages of the book, especially if the book is old or valuable.

In conclusion, each of these drying methods has its pros and cons, and the choice of method depends on your needs and preferences. Silica gel is a fast and effective option, but it can be expensive and messy. Flower presses are effective and long-lasting, but they can be slow to dry (this is a must-have tool to preserve your wedding blooms). Books are cost-effective and easy to use, but they can take a long time to dry and can damage the pages of the book. Consider your specific needs and choose the method that best fits your requirements.

Turning dried flowers into confetti:

- ▶ Cut and slice method

To turn dried flowers into confetti, start by choosing the dried flowers you want to use. Make sure they are completely dry and free of moisture. Next, carefully cut or tear the flowers into small pieces that are suitable for use as confetti. You can use scissors or a paper cutter to achieve the desired size.

Once the flowers have been cut into pieces, place them into a container and store them until you are ready to use them as confetti.

- ▶ Grinding method

An alternative method to turn dried and pressed flowers into confetti is to use a food processor or a coffee grinder. This method is especially suitable if you have many dried flowers that need to be broken down into small pieces.

Simply place a small quantity of the dried flowers into the food processor or coffee grinder and pulse until the flowers are broken down into confetti-sized pieces. This method is fast and efficient and ensures the flowers are cut into uniform pieces for a consistent look.

It is important to note that this method may generate some dust, so it is advisable to do it in a well-ventilated area and wear a mask if necessary.

- ▶ Crushing method

Crushing the dried and pressed flowers is a simple and straightforward way to turn them into confetti. This method involves simply taking the dried and pressed flowers and crushing them into smaller pieces using your hands or a rolling pin.

This method is particularly suitable if you only have a small number of flowers and don't mind having a more natural, rustic look to your confetti. You can also use this method to create a mixture of sizes by crushing some of the flowers into finer pieces and leaving others in larger pieces.

The crushed dried flowers can then be stored in a container until you are ready to use them as confetti. This method is cost-effective, easy, and allows you to create a unique look for your event.

STORING YOUR FLOWER CONFETTI

Storing your dried confetti flowers before the special event is an important step to ensure they are in the best condition on the day.

To store your dried flowers, choose an airtight container, such as a jar or plastic bag, and make sure it is completely dry. Avoid storing your dried flowers in damp or humid environments, as this can cause them to mold or deteriorate.

Keep them in a cool, dry place away from direct sunlight and away from strong odors as well. You can also add a packet of silica gel to absorb any excess moisture and help keep your dried flowers fresh.

With proper storage, your dried confetti flowers will be ready and waiting for your special event, adding a touch of beauty and joy to the occasion.

Well, folks, let me tell you, drying flowers for confetti is a fantastic way to add some extra pizzazz to your celebration. It's like adding a cherry on top of a sundae; it just takes the whole experience to the next level. And the best part is that it's not rocket science.

In this chapter, we've covered all the important bits and pieces, from why dried flowers make better confetti than fresh flowers to which flowers work best and the various methods of drying them. We've also had a chat about turning those dried blooms into beautiful confetti and how to store them before the big day.

So, whether you're looking to add a touch of romance or just want to bring some nature into your celebration, drying flowers for confetti is the way to go. Just remember, with a little patience and TLC, you'll have confetti that will make all your guests smile and dance the night away.

CRAFT IDEAS FOR PRESSED FLOWER PROJECTS

"The violets in the mountains have broken the rocks." - Tennessee Williams

*A*re you looking for fun and creative ways to display your pressed flowers? Look no further. In this chapter, we'll share with you some unique and exciting ways to show off your dried floral collection.

From resin coasters to greeting cards, there's something for everyone. So, if you're ready to get creative and bring your pressed flowers to life, keep reading. You'll be amazed at the beautiful and practical projects you can achieve with these colorful pieces of nature.

You will need pressed flowers for all the ideas. If you don't already have them, you'll need to press them first. You can use a wooden flower press or press them in books. The flowers usually take about two to three weeks to fully dry.

RESIN COASTERS

Resin coasters are a unique and practical way to showcase your pressed flowers. All you need is a silicone mold, resin, and your pressed flowers.

These coasters will elevate your table setup and protect the tabletops from damage at the same time.

How to make the coasters:

Step 1:
Mix the resin and hardener according to the ratio given on the bottle.

Step 2:
Pour a thin layer of the resin mixture into a silicon coaster mold.

Step 3:

Once the first layer of resin dries, add the pressed flowers on top in your desired arrangement.

Step 4:

Add another layer of resin and let it dry.

Step 5:

Add a final layer of resin and fill to the top of the mold.

Once the final layer dries, your flower coaster is ready to use. These make particularly great gifts for nature lovers.

PRESSED FLOWER BOOKMARKS

If you're a reader, then you'll love using pressed flower bookmarks. They add a personal touch to your reading experience and make it that much more special. Plus, they're super easy to make.

All you need is a piece of cardstock, a ribbon, and your pressed flowers.

How to make bookmarks using pressed flowers:

Step 1:

Take a thick piece of paper in your desired color and cut it to the shape of your bookmark.

Step 2:

Place the dried flowers in the arrangement you want within the bookmark.

Step 3:

Once the positions are fixed, use a paintbrush to apply mod

podge on the paper and place the flower according to the arrangement.

Step 4:

After the first layer dries, apply another layer of mod podge on top of the flowers to secure them.

You can do this with both sides of the bookmark or just on one side. When the Mod Podge dries, you will have a bookmark showcasing beautifully preserved flowers.

CANDLE HOLDERS

Candle holders: Add a touch of nature to your home with pressed flower candle holders.

You will need small glass jars (like baby food jars), pressed flowers, strong adhesive that dries clear (e.g., Mod Podge), and tealight candles.

Step 1:

Gather your materials. Make sure you have all the necessary supplies before starting your project.

Step 2:

Clean your glass jars. Make sure to wash and dry your glass jars thoroughly. This will help the adhesive to stick better.

Step 3:

Arrange your flowers on the outside of the jar. Experiment with different arrangements and choose the one you like best.

Step 4:

Glue your flowers onto the jar. Use a strong adhesive, such as Mod Podge glue, to secure your flowers in place. Once dry, paint another layer of glue over the flowers to seal and secure them.

Step 5:
Let the glue dry. Allow the glue to dry completely before moving on to the next step. This can take anywhere from a few hours to a full day, depending on the adhesive you're using.

Step 6:
Add a tealight candle. Once the glue is fully dry, place a tealight candle inside the jar. Light the candle and enjoy your beautiful, pressed flower candle holder.

And that's it. In just a few simple steps, you can transform a small glass jar into a beautiful and unique candle holder. These make great gifts and add a touch of nature to any home.

SUPER EASY SUNCATCHERS

Brighten up any window with pressed flower suncatchers. All you need are some clear plastic sheets, pressed flowers, a hole punch, glue, and scissors.

Making suncatchers:

Step 1:
Press your flowers.

Step 2:
Cut out a shape from the plastic. Use scissors to cut out a shape from the clear plastic sheets. You can choose any

shape you like, such as a circle, star, or heart.

Step 3:
Punch a hole at the top. Use a hole punch to create a hole at the top of your plastic shape. This is where you'll hang your suncatcher.

Step 4:
Arrange your flowers. Experiment with different arrangements and choose the one you like best.

Step 5:
Glue your flowers onto the plastic. Use a strong adhesive that dries clear.

Step 6:
Let the glue dry. Allow the glue to dry completely before moving on to the next step.

Step 7:
Hang your suncatcher.

Once the glue is fully dry, hang your suncatcher in a sunny window using the hole at the top. Enjoy the beautiful display of colors as the sun shines through your pressed flowers.

GREETING CARDS

Make someone's day with a handmade greeting card featuring pressed flowers. Simply press your flowers and arrange them on a blank card. You can also write a message or a quote in the center of the card.

These cards are perfect for any occasion and are sure to be appreciated.

FLOATING FRAMES

Floating frames are perfect for displaying pressed flowers because they allow the flowers to be seen from both sides. This makes them a unique and eye-catching display option. The clear plastic also allows the natural colors of the flowers to shine through, creating a beautiful and vibrant display.

To make floating frames, you will need pressed flowers, clear plastic sheets, glue that dries clear, scissors, and a picture frame.

Step 1:
Cut out a piece of clear plastic. Use scissors to cut out a piece of clear plastic that is slightly larger than the opening of your picture frame. This way, you won't have to glue the flowers to the glass itself.

Step 2:
Arrange your flowers. Experiment with different arrangements and choose the one you like best.

Step 3:
Secure the flowers to the plastic. Use just a small dot of glue to secure the flowers to the plastic sheet. One tip I can share is that I like to use a toothpick for that. Then press the bloom gently with your finger to make sure it's fixed.

Step 4:
Insert the plastic into the frame. Place the plastic sheet with the pressed flowers into the picture frame, making sure it's centered.

Step 5:

Close the frame.

Step 6:

Display your floating frame. Hang your floating frame on your wall and enjoy the beautiful display of pressed flowers.

As you can see, there are many unique and creative ways to display and use your dried floral collection. From resin coasters to suncatchers, there's something for everyone. I hope I've inspired you to get creative and make something special with your pressed flowers.

Remember, the best part about crafting with pressed flowers is that you can customize your projects to fit your style and taste. Don't be afraid to get creative and try something new. Whether you're looking to add some beauty to your home or create a special gift for someone, these crafts are sure to impress. So, gather your materials and get crafting! You'll be amazed at the beautiful and practical projects you can make with these colorful pieces of nature. Happy crafting!

TOP FIVE CRAFTY GIFT IDEAS FOR PRESSED FLOWER LOVERS

"Flowers always look up to the sun because it makes them grow. So choose to look up to the positive things in life, it'll make you grow too." - Mother Nature

Choosing the best gift option for a fellow craft-loving person can be a REAL task! Especially if their art revolves around some DIY fresh flower pressing! Do you want your flower pressing friend to swoon over a perfect present, but you can't wrap your head around the best present for the arts and craft buff?

Stay tuned because by the end of this chapter, you will have five unique gift ideas for your pressed flower-loving buddy!

WOODEN FLOWER PRESS

The most common and traditional flower pressing method is to use a wooden flower press. And all flower pressing enthusiasts will surely receive a wooden press with bright smiles and twinkling eyes!

Especially the <u>Berstuk flower press,</u> a DIY, easy, and all-in-one kit for juicing some fresh flowers! Your friend is bound to love it because it comes in an attractive gift box. It makes an amazing gift for people to have a cool kit on the go. The DIY flower press is super compact, stylish, and light.

SILICA GEL FOR FLOWER PRESSING

Silica gel for flower drying is the perfect gift for anyone who loves pressing and drying flowers. Not only is it a practical and useful item, but it also shows that you care about their passion and want to help them preserve their hard work.

When it comes to drying flowers, silica gel is an essential tool that absorbs excess moisture and helps to keep the flowers looking fresh and vibrant. It's a gift that keeps on giving, as it can be used over and over again for countless flower pressing projects.

In short, silica gel for flower drying is a thoughtful, useful, and much-appreciated gift for anyone who loves this craft.

TWEEZERS, SCALPEL, AND GARDEN SCISSORS

Really? Tweezers and a scalpel for an art and craft lover? Doesn't make much sense!

Well, tweezers and scalpels can come in handy when pressing flowers. The floral cuttings need to be handled lightly and with care, and tweezers help pick up delicate pieces efficiently. Also, curved tweezers make it easier to position pressed blooms.

And a scalpel? I know what you are thinking. Isn't that a gift you should give a doctor? Well, true! But flower pressing methods also include making vertical incisions to cut the flower into equal halves.

Garden scissors are just a must-have for anyone who deals with flowers. No question about that. These are perfect, and they look fab too.

If you want to make your friend happy, give them this "out of the box" item! Be ready to be surprised when they skip with joy when receiving these tools!

$20 FLORIST GIFT CARD

If you're not sure what specific items your friend needs for their flower pressing hobby, consider getting them a $20 gift card for their favorite local florist.

Gift cards are the best and most well-received option. You buy a card and give it to someone to use WHENEVER they need it. A $20 florist card is a great idea.

Local florists also create some pretty amazing DIY floral beauties that your friend is surely going to love. This way, they will have lots more blooms to press and art to create. The thing about this option is to let them go and pick the flowers they love the most so they can press them. Don't forget to add that note in the little envelope.

SPECIALIST FLOWER PRESS PAPER

Blotting paper for flower pressing is a unique and perfect gift idea for any flower preservation artist. If you know someone who loves to press and dry flowers, chances are they can never have enough blotting paper on hand.

These sheets are essential for absorbing excess moisture and helping to preserve the color of pressed flowers, making them a must-have item for any flower pressing enthusiast.

Not only is blotting paper a practical and useful gift, but it's also a thoughtful and considerate choice that shows you care about your friend's passion and want to support them in their craft. Plus, with its versatility and convenience, blotting paper is a gift that will be much appreciated and put to good use.

In conclusion, if you're looking for the perfect gift for a pressed flower lover, you can't go wrong with any of the options listed in this chapter. From a wooden flower press and silica gel for preserving flowers to tweezers and scalpels, a florist gift card, or blotting paper, these gift ideas are sure to delight any crafty nature enthusiast.

Whether you choose a traditional or more unexpected item, your friend is sure to appreciate the thought and effort you put into finding something that aligns with their interests and passions.

So, don't hesitate; show your support for your friend's love of flower pressing with one of these unique and enticing gift ideas. They'll be sure to thank you with bright smiles and twinkling eyes.

COMMON CHALLENGES IN FLOWER PRESSING

"To plant a garden is to believe in tomorrow." - Audrey Hepburn

*F*lower pressing is a delightful journey filled with beauty and creativity. However, it can also come with a fair share of challenges. Faded colors, mold growth, browned petals, and delicate flowers getting crushed are a few of these obstacles. But don't worry, as every problem comes with a solution, and I'm here to share a few to help you perfect your art.

1. FADED COLORS

Color fading is one of the most common challenges when pressing flowers. The transformation from fresh blooms to a pressed masterpiece can sometimes cause the vibrant colors to lose their intensity. The reasons for this could be many. For example, flowers naturally lose some color during the drying process. Additionally, exposure to sunlight and air can further cause the colors to fade.

To combat this:

▸ Always use fresh flowers. Picking flowers in full bloom ensures their pigments are at their peak. Aim to pick your flowers on a dry, sunny day, after the morning dew has evaporated, to avoid any excess moisture that could accelerate color loss.
▸ Press your flowers as soon as possible after picking them. The less time between picking and pressing, the more vibrant the colors are likely to remain. Delays can lead to wilting and color loss.

▸ Store your pressed flowers properly. Keep them in a cool, dark place away from direct sunlight, as ultraviolet rays can cause colors to fade.

2. MOLD GROWTH

Mold is a common issue when pressing flowers, and it usually occurs when flowers aren't dry enough before or during pressing.

To prevent this:

▸ Pick flowers at the right time. When flowers are picked after the morning dew has evaporated, they carry less moisture, minimizing the risk of mold.
▸ Choose your pressing materials wisely. Berstuk Blotting paper or other papers specifically designed to absorb moisture can help in reducing the risk of mold.
▸ Change pressing materials when necessary. If you're pressing a particularly moist flower, you might need to replace the pressing paper midway through the process to keep the moisture levels low and prevent mold.

3. FLOWERS TURNING BROWN

Sometimes, flowers may turn brown during pressing, which can be due to oxidation, like how an apple turns brown when exposed to air.

To avoid this:

- ▸ Use acid-free paper. Regular paper can contain acids that speed up oxidation, causing flowers to brown. Acid-free paper or blotting paper can help avoid this issue.
- ▸ Dry your flowers quickly. The quicker the flowers dry, the less likely they are to brown. If you notice your flowers frequently browning, consider adopting a quicker drying method, such as a microwave flower press.

4. PETALS OVERLAPPING OR FOLDING

Delicate petals can sometimes fold or overlap each other, which can distort the beauty of the pressed flower.

Here's how you can deal with it:

- ▸ Arrange your flowers carefully before pressing. Take your time to arrange the petals as you want them to appear when dried. Using a flat object like a butter knife can help you adjust the petals without damaging them.
- ▸ Close your press or book slowly when pressing. This gives the petals time to adjust and flatten rather than folding over each other.

5. DELICATE FLOWERS GETTING CRUSHED

Some flowers are particularly delicate and can be easily damaged during pressing.

To protect them:

▶ Consider using a pressing cloth. This can provide additional protection for delicate flowers, cushioning them and helping to distribute the pressing weight evenly.

▶ Be careful not to over-tighten your press. Apply just enough pressure to flatten the flowers, but not so much that it damages them. The Berstuk flower press gives you that level of control so that you can tighten the wing nuts daily for perfect pressing.

Remember, as you deepen your practice of flower pressing, challenges will occur, but they are opportunities for learning and refining your craft.

FAQ – QUICK REFERENCE GUIDE TO FLOWER PRESSING

"When a flower doesn't bloom you fix the environment in which it grows, not the flower." - Alexander Den Heijer

*I*n this chapter, we address some of the most frequently asked questions about flower pressing. Whether you're just beginning your journey into this beautiful art or already have some experience, this guide aims to provide quick, easy-to-understand answers to your queries.

1. CAN ALL FLOWERS BE PRESSED?

While nearly all flowers can be pressed, the results can vary depending on the flower's thickness and moisture content. Thin and flat flowers like pansies or violets press well. More robust or fleshy flowers, such as roses or orchids, may need to be pressed petal by petal, or they may require longer pressing times.

2. WHAT IS THE BEST TIME TO PICK FLOWERS FOR PRESSING?

The ideal time to pick flowers is in the morning after the dew has dried but before the harsh midday sun. Flowers picked during this time tend to retain their color better. Also, it's best to choose flowers that are in their prime or just about to bloom fully.

3. WHY ARE MY PRESSED FLOWERS TURNING BROWN?

Flowers can turn brown for a variety of reasons. It might be because the flowers were not fresh when picked, they contained too much moisture when pressed, or they were exposed to heat for an extended period. Sometimes, certain flowers naturally fade or darken due to their inherent properties.

4. HOW LONG SHOULD I LEAVE THE FLOWERS IN THE PRESS?

Typically, flowers should be left in the press for two to three weeks. However, this can vary depending on the type and thickness of the flower. For some dense or moist flowers, it might take longer.

5. HOW CAN I PREVENT MOLD ON MY PRESSED FLOWERS?

Mold on pressed flowers is often a result of too much moisture. To prevent this, make sure your flowers are completely dry before pressing. Also, use absorbent paper and change it out frequently if you're pressing a particularly moist flower.

6. WHY ARE MY PRESSED FLOWERS LOSING COLOR?

Color fading in pressed flowers can be due to several factors, including the natural pigmentation of the flowers, exposure to sunlight, or excessive heat during the drying process. Using acid-free paper can help reduce color loss, and storing your pressed flowers in a dark, cool place can also help preserve their color.

7. CAN PRESSED FLOWERS BE USED IN RESIN?

Absolutely! Pressed flowers are often used in resin to create beautiful items like jewelry, bookmarks, paperweights, and more. Ensure your flowers are completely dry before embedding them in resin to prevent bubbles or discoloration.

8. HOW CAN I MAKE MY PRESSED FLOWERS LAST LONGER?

Sealing your pressed flowers with a UV-resistant spray or fixative can help them last longer. Also, keep them out of direct sunlight and high-humidity areas. Remember, pressed flowers are delicate, so handle them with care to preserve their beauty.

9. CAN I PRESS FLOWERS THAT HAVE SENTIMENTAL VALUE, LIKE A WEDDING BOUQUET?

Certainly! Pressing flowers from special occasions is a wonderful way to create lasting memories. Just remember, the sooner you press the flowers after the event, the better the results will be.

10. HOW CAN I DISPLAY MY PRESSED FLOWERS?

Pressed flowers can be displayed in numerous creative ways. You can make wall art, greeting cards, bookmarks, or even decorate photo frames or lampshades. The possibilities are endless.

Remember, flower pressing is as much a science as it is an art. It may take a bit of trial and error to get it just right. So, stay patient, keep experimenting, and, most importantly, enjoy the process!

CONCLUSION: THE JOURNEY CONTINUES

*D*ear blooming artists

We've journeyed together through the enchanting world of flower pressing, from its history and basic techniques to more intricate methods and creative applications. Each chapter, each word, and each tip in this book was written with love and care, driven by my passion for this art form and the desire to share it with all of you.

But our journey doesn't end here.

The magic of flower pressing extends beyond the petals and leaves we've carefully pressed and preserved. It grows, much like a flower itself, into a beautiful community of artists, hobbyists, and flower lovers. A community where we can share our experiences, inspire each other, celebrate our triumphs, and learn from our setbacks.

My goal is to create a space that resembles a field in full bloom: diverse, vibrant, and united by a shared love for flowers and the art we create with them. A space where every member is like a unique flower contributing to the beauty of the whole garden. A space where we're more than just fellow artists; we're a family.

So, let's continue to inspire and learn from each other. Share your pressed flower work with me and tag me on Instagram @flowerpresstips. Let's show the world the beauty we've preserved, the memories we've imprinted on petals, and the passion and patience we've poured into our art. Let's invite others to join our family, share in our joy, and fall in love with the art of flower pressing, just as we have.

Remember, every flower has a story to tell, and every pressing is a page in your unique tale. Keep pressing, keep exploring, and keep growing. And most importantly, keep sharing your stories because your journey adds a unique and invaluable bloom to our growing garden of flower preservation artists.

Thank you for embarking on this journey with me. I look forward to seeing your blooming masterpieces and hearing your stories. See you in our beautiful flower field.

Lots of love,

Printed in Great Britain
by Amazon